Congressional
Research
Service

Country-of-Origin Labeling for Foods and the WTO Trade Dispute on Meat Labeling

Remy Jurenas
Specialist in Agricultural Policy

Joel L. Greene
Analyst in Agricultural Policy

July 3, 2012

Congressional Research Service
7-5700
www.crs.gov
RS22955

CRS Report for Congress ————————————
Prepared for Members and Committees of Congress

Summary

Most retail food stores are now required to inform consumers about the country of origin of fresh fruits and vegetables, fish, shellfish, peanuts, pecans, macadamia nuts, ginseng, and ground and muscle cuts of beef, pork, lamb, chicken, and goat. The rules are required by the 2002 farm bill (P.L. 107-171) as amended by the 2008 farm bill (P.L. 110-246). Other U.S. laws have required such labeling, but only for imported food products already pre-packaged for consumers. The final rule to implement COOL took effect on March 16, 2009.

Both the authorization and implementation of country-of-origin labeling (COOL) by the U.S. Department of Agriculture's Agricultural Marketing Service have been controversial. Much attention has focused on the labeling rules that now apply to meat and meat products. A number of livestock and food industry groups continue to oppose COOL as costly and unnecessary. They and the main livestock exporters to the United States—Canada and Mexico—view the requirement as trade-distorting. Others, including some cattle and consumer groups, maintain that Americans want and deserve to know the origin of their foods, and point out that many U.S. trading partners have their own import labeling requirements.

Less than one year after the COOL rules took effect, Canada and Mexico used the World Trade Organization's (WTO's) trade dispute resolution process to challenge some features that apply to labeling meat. Both countries argued that COOL has a trade-distorting impact by reducing the value and number of cattle and hogs shipped to the U.S. market. For this reason, they argued that COOL violates WTO trade commitments agreed to by the United States. On November 18, 2011, a WTO dispute settlement (DS) panel found that (1) COOL treats imported livestock less favorably than like U.S. livestock (particularly in the labeling of beef and pork muscle cuts), and (2) COOL does not meet its objective to provide complete information to consumers on the origin of meat products. The panel reached these conclusions by examining the economic effects of the measures taken by U.S. livestock producers and meat processors to implement COOL, and by accepting arguments that the way meat is labeled to indicate where the multiple steps of livestock birth, raising, and slaughtering occurred is confusing.

On March 23, 2012, the United States appealed the panel report to the WTO Appellate Body (AB). On June 29, 2012, the AB upheld the DS panel's finding that the COOL measure treats imported Canadian cattle and hogs, and imported Mexican cattle, less favorably than like domestic livestock, because of its record-keeping and verification requirements. The AB, however, reversed the panel's finding that COOL does not fulfill its legitimate objective to provide consumers with information on origin. The Obama Administration welcomed the AB's affirmation of the U.S. right to adopt labeling requirements to inform consumers on the origin of the meat they purchase, but did not signal what steps might be considered to address the 'less favorable treatment' finding. Participants in the U.S. livestock sector had mixed reactions, reflecting the heated debate on COOL that occurred over the last decade. Two consumer groups expressed concern that this WTO decision further undermines U.S. consumer protections.

If the United States decides to bring COOL into compliance with the AB finding, WTO rules call for that to occur within a reasonable period of time. Options would be to consider regulatory and/or statutory changes to the COOL regulations and/or law. If the United States does not comply, Canada and Mexico would have the right to seek compensation or retaliate against imports from the United States.

Contents

Figures

Tables

Appendixes

Contacts

Overview

Since the 1930s, U.S. tariff law has required almost all imports to carry labels so that the "ultimate purchaser," usually the retail consumer, can determine their country of origin. However, certain products, including a number of agricultural commodities in their "natural" state, such as meats, fruits and vegetables, were excluded (see **Appendix A** for a description of this and two other food labeling laws dealing with the display of country of origin on imported products). For almost as many decades, various farm and consumer groups have pressed Congress to end one or more of these exceptions, arguing that U.S. consumers have a right to know where all of their food comes from and that, given a choice, they would purchase the domestic version. This would strengthen demand and prices for U.S. farmers and ranchers, it was argued.

Opponents of ending these exceptions to country-of-origin labeling (COOL) contended that there was little or no real evidence that consumers want such information and that industry compliance costs would far outweigh any potential benefits to producers or consumers. Such opponents, including some farm and food marketing groups, argued that mandatory COOL for meats, produce, or other agricultural commodities was a form of protectionism that would undermine U.S. efforts to reduce foreign barriers to trade in the global economy. COOL supporters countered that it was unfair to exempt agricultural commodities from the labeling requirements that U.S. importers of almost all other products already must meet, and that major U.S. trading partners impose their own COOL requirements for imported meats, produce, and other foods.

Legislation

With passage of the 2002 farm bill (P.L. 107-171, §10816), retail-level COOL was to become mandatory for fresh fruits and vegetables, beef, pork, lamb, seafood, and peanuts, starting September 30, 2004. Continuing controversy over the new requirements within the food and agricultural industry led Congress to postpone full implementation. The FY2004 Omnibus Appropriations Act (P.L. 108-199) postponed COOL—except for seafood—until September 30, 2006; the FY2006 Agriculture Appropriations Act (P.L. 109-97) further postponed it until September 30, 2008.

During deliberations on the 2008 farm bill, the interest groups most affected by COOL reached consensus on various changes intended to ease what they viewed to be some of the more onerous provisions of the 2002 COOL law. Provisions dealing with record-keeping requirements, the factors to be considered for labeling U.S. and non-U.S. origin products, and penalties for noncompliance were modified. These amendments were incorporated into P.L. 110-246, Section 11002. The enacted 2008 farm bill required that COOL take effect on September 30, 2008, and added goat meat, chicken, macadamia nuts, pecans, and ginseng as commodities covered by mandatory COOL. (See **Appendix B** for a timeline of key COOL developments.)

USDA Regulations and Secretary's Statement to Implement COOL

The final rule to implement the COOL requirements for all covered commodities was issued by the U.S. Department of Agriculture's (USDA's) Agricultural Marketing Service (AMS) during the final days of the Bush Administration in January 2009.[1] It included changes to the interim rule published in August 2008 that some had criticized as watering down the COOL statute (see "Changes Made from Interim Rule to Final Rule"). In February 2009, the Secretary of Agriculture announced that the final rule would take effect as planned on March 16, 2009. However, he also urged affected industries to adopt—voluntarily—additional changes that, he asserted, would provide more specific origin information to consumers and more closely adhere to the intent of the COOL law (see section titled "Vilsack Letter" for details).

Costs and Benefits

COOL supporters argued that numerous studies show that consumers want country-of-origin labeling and would pay extra for it. Analysis accompanying USDA's interim and final rules concluded that, while benefits are difficult to quantify, it appears they will be small and will accrue mainly to consumers who desire such information. A Colorado State University economist suggested that consumers might be willing to pay a premium for "COOL meat" from the United States, but only if they perceive U.S. meat to be safer and of higher quality than foreign meat.[2] USDA earlier had estimated that purchases of (i.e., demand for) covered commodities would have to increase by 1% to 5% for benefits to cover COOL costs, but added that such increases were not anticipated. Data from several economic studies that aimed to model COOL impacts appear to fall within this range.[3]

Critics of mandatory COOL have argued that large compliance costs will more than offset any consumer benefits. USDA's analysis of its final rule estimates first-year implementation costs to be approximately $2.6 billion for those affected. Of the total, each commodity producer would bear an average estimated cost of $370, intermediary firms (such as wholesalers or processors) $48,219 each, and retailers $254,685 each. The USDA analysis also includes estimates of record-keeping costs and of food sector economic losses due to the rule.

COOL's Meat Labeling Challenged in the WTO

Meat labeling proved to be the most contentious of COOL requirements, leading Canada and Mexico to challenge COOL using the World Trade Organization's (WTO's) dispute settlement process. They were concerned that normal livestock trade flows would be disrupted in response to the COOL regulations and questioned COOL's legality under international trade rules. After

---

[1] USDA, January 12, 2009, "USDA Issues Final Rule On Mandatory Country of Origin Labeling," available at http://www.usda.gov/wps/portal/usda/usdahome?printable=true&contentidonly=true&contentid=2009/01/0006.xml; and *Federal Register*, January 15, 2009, pp. 2658-2707. This final rule replaced both the April 4, 2005, interim final rule for seafood, and the August 1, 2008, interim final rule (*Federal Register*, pp. 45106-45151) for all other covered commodities. An AMS fact sheet on the final rule, including a summary of changes from the interim final rules and estimates on COOL implementation costs, is available at http://www.ams.usda.gov/AMSv1.0/getfile?dDocName= STELPRDC5074847.

[2] Wendy J. Umberger, "Will Consumers Pay a Premium for Country-of-Origin Labeled Meat?," *Choices*, 4th quarter 2004, http://www.choicesmagazine.org/2004-4/cool/2004-4-04.htm.

[3] Gary W. Brewster et al., "Who Will Bear the Costs of Country-of-Origin Labeling?," available at http://www.choicesmagazine.org/2004-4/cool/2004-4-02.htm; Daniel D. Hanselka et al., "Demand Shifts in Beef Associated with Country-of-Origin Labeling to Minimize Losses in Social Welfare," *Choices*, 4th quarter 2004, http://www.choicesmagazine.org/2004-4/cool/2004-4-03.htm; and Alejandro Plastina and Konstantinos Giannakis, "Market and Welfare Effects of Mandatory Country-of-Origin Labeling in the U.S. Specialty Crops Sector," American Agricultural Economics Association Annual Meeting, Portland, Oregon, 2007.

weighing available options, the Obama Administration decided to appeal the WTO's adverse findings issued in late 2011 on some of COOL's provisions. If the U.S. appeal is not successful, Congress may step in to amend the COOL statute or to advocate regulatory changes to bring this labeling program into compliance with WTO rules.

Key Provisions of COOL

Mandatory country-of-origin labeling:

- *applies* to ground and muscle cuts of beef, lamb, and pork, farm-raised and wild fish and shellfish, peanuts, "perishable agricultural commodities" as defined by the Perishable Agricultural Commodities Act (i.e., fresh and frozen fruits and vegetables), goat meat, chicken, pecans, macadamia nuts, and ginseng (these are referred to as "covered commodities");[4]

- *exempts* these items if they are an ingredient in a processed food;

- *covers* only those retailers that annually purchase at least $230,000 of perishable agricultural commodities,[5] and requires them to inform consumers of origin "by means of a label, stamp, mark, placard, or other clear and visible sign on the covered commodity or on the package, display, holding unit, or bin containing the commodity at the final point of sale"; and

- *exempts* from these labeling requirements such "food service establishments" as restaurants, cafeterias, bars, and similar facilities that prepare and sell foods to the public.

Defining and Labeling Origin for Meats

In designating country of origin, difficulties arise when products—particularly meats—are produced in multiple countries. For example, beef might be from an animal that was born and fed in Canada, but slaughtered and processed in the United States. Likewise, products from several different countries often are mixed, such as for ground beef. For covered red meats and chicken, the COOL law:

- *permits* the U.S. origin label to be used only on meats from animals that were exclusively born, raised, and slaughtered in the United States, with an exception for those animals present here before July 15, 2008;

- *permits* meats or chicken with multiple countries of origin to be labeled as being from all of the countries in which the animals may have been born, raised, or slaughtered;

---

[4] A slightly different COOL requirement applies to packaged honey if it bears any official USDA certificate, mark, or statement with respect to quality and grade. It was added by Section 10402 of the 2008 farm bill (P.L. 110-246) to the Agricultural Marketing Act, and took effect on October 6, 2009. For more information, see http://www.ams.usda.gov/ AMSv1.0/ams.fetchTemplateData.do?startIndex=1&startIndex=2&startIndex=1&startIndex=2&template= TemplateN&navID=ProcessedFVUpdates&rightNav1=&topNav=&leftNav=&page=ProcessedFVUpdates& resultType=&acct=procsdgrdcert.

[5] The COOL statute uses by reference this definition of "retailer" laid out in the Perishable Agricultural Commodities Act to identify those retailers required to comply with COOL requirements.

- *requires* meat or chicken from animals imported for immediate U.S. slaughter to be labeled as from both the country the animal came from and the United States;

- *requires* products from animals not born, raised, or slaughtered in the United States to be labeled with their correct country(ies) of origin; and

- *requires*, for ground meat and chicken products, that the label list all countries of origin, or all "reasonably possible" countries of origin.

Because these statutory requirements are at the heart of the ongoing WTO dispute case, **Table 1** traces the progression of statutory language to implementing regulations to the retail labels to be used for each of these five categories.

Changes Made from Interim Rule to Final Rule

The meat labeling requirements have proven to be among the most complex and controversial areas of rulemaking, in large part because of the steps that U.S. feeding operations and packing plants must adopt to segregate, hold, and slaughter foreign-origin livestock separately from U.S. livestock. After AMS issued the interim rules in August 2008, many retailers and meat processors reportedly planned to use the "catch-all" multiple countries of origin label on as much meat as possible—even products that would qualify for the U.S.-only label, because it was both permitted and the easiest requirement to meet. COOL supporters objected that the label would be overused, undermining the intent of COOL (i.e., to distinguish between U.S. and non-U.S. meats).[6] In an effort to balance the concerns of both sides, USDA issued a statement attempting to clarify its August 2008 interim rule, stating that meats derived from both U.S.- and non-U.S.-origin animals may carry a mixed-origin claim (e.g., "Product of U.S., Canada, and Mexico"), but that the mixed-origin label cannot be used if only U.S.-origin meat was produced on a production day.[7]

The final (January 2009) rule attempted to further clarify the "multiple countries of origin" language. For example, muscle cut products of exclusively U.S. origin along with those from foreign-born animals, if commingled for slaughter on a single production day, can continue to qualify for a combined U.S. and non-U.S. label. "It was never the intent of the Agency [AMS] for the majority of product eligible to bear a U.S. origin declaration to bear a multiple origin destination. The Agency made additional modifications for clarity," AMS stated in material accompanying the rule.[8]

The clarifying changes failed to mollify some. The National Farmers Union continued to view this portion of the rule as a "loophole that would allow meat packers to use a multiple countries, or NAFTA [North American Free Trade Agreement] label, rather than labeling U.S. products as products of the United States" and stated "[t]his is misleading to consumers".[9] Seven senators highlighted similar concerns, stating that it would allow "meatpackers to put a multiple country of origin label on products that are exclusively U.S. products as well as those that are foreign." They characterized the final rule as defeating COOL's primary purpose to provide "clear, accurate and

---

[6] *Cattle Buyers Weekly*, August 4, 2008; and *Food Chemical News*, September 15, 2008.

[7] AMS, "Country of Origin Labeling (COOL) Frequently Asked Questions," September 26, 2008, http://www.ams.usda.gov/AMSv1.0/getfile?dDocName=STELPRDC5071922.

[8] USDA, AMS, January 12, 2009, fact sheet on the mandatory COOL final rule, p. 5, http://www.ams.usda.gov/AMSv1.0/getfile?dDocName=STELPRDC5074847.

[9] "NFU Statement: USDA Issues Final Rule for COOL," January 12, 2009, http://nfu.org/news/news-archives/2009-news/86-agriculture-programs/198-nfu-statement-usda-issues-final-rule-for-cool.

truthful information" to U.S. consumers, and hoped the rules will be revised "to close these loopholes."[10]

Vilsack Letter

To address these views to comply with an Obama White House directive that all agencies review recent regulations issued by the outgoing Administration, Secretary of Agriculture Vilsack in a February 20, 2009, letter urged industry representatives to voluntarily adopt three suggested labeling changes in order to provide more useful information to consumers than the final rule itself might imply, and to better meet congressional intent. These dealt with the labeling of meat products with multiple countries of origin, a reduction in the time allowance for labeling ground meat held in inventory, and exemptions to the rules for processed products.

On labeling for multiple countries of origin, he stated that

> processors should voluntarily include information about what production step occurred in each country when multiple countries appear on the label. For example, animals born and raised in Country X and slaughtered in Country Y might be labeled as "Born and Raised in Country X and Slaughtered in Country Y." Animals born in Country X but raised and slaughtered in Country Y might be labeled as "Born in Country X and Raised and Slaughtered in Country Y."

Vilsack's letter noted that the final rule allows a label for ground meat to bear the name of a country even if the meat from that country was not present in a processor's inventory in the preceding 60-day period. Noting that this allows for labeling this product "in a way that does not clearly indicate [its] country of origin," the Secretary asked processors to reduce this time allowance to 10 days, stating that this "would enhance the credibility of the label." (See also "Scope of Coverage.")

Secretary Vilsack also stated that USDA would closely monitor industry compliance to determine whether "additional rulemaking may be necessary to provide consumers with adequate information."[11] His letter was widely viewed as an effort to address the concerns of COOL adherents without reopening the rule and thereby attracting renewed criticism from the meat industry and U.S. trading partners.

Defining Origin for Other Covered Commodities

For perishable agricultural commodities, ginseng, peanuts, pecans, and macadamia nuts, retailers may only claim U.S. origin if the product was exclusively produced in the United States. However, a U.S. state, region, or locality designation is a sufficient U.S. identifier (e.g., Idaho potatoes). For farm-raised fish and shellfish, a U.S.-labeled product must be derived exclusively from fish or shellfish hatched, raised, harvested, and processed in the United States; wild fish and shellfish must be derived exclusively from those harvested either in U.S. waters or by a U.S. flagged vessel, and processed in the United States or on a U.S. vessel. Also, labels must differentiate between wild and farm-raised fish and shellfish.

---

[10] Letter to Secretary of Agriculture Tom Vilsack, February 3, 2009, http://web.archive.org/web/20090226012829/ http://dorgan.senate.gov/newsroom/extras/020309vilsack.pdf.

[11] USDA, "Vilsack Announces Implementation of Country of Origin Labeling Law," February 20, 2009, http://www.usda.gov/wps/portal/usda/usdahome?printable=true&contentidonly=true&contentid=2009/02/0045.xml. His letter is available at http://www.usda.gov/documents/0220_IndustryLetterCOOL.pdf.

Scope of Coverage

Consumers may not find country-of-origin labels on much more of the food they buy, due to COOL's statutory and regulatory exemptions. First, as noted, all restaurants and other food service providers are exempt, as are all retail grocery stores that buy less than $230,000 a year in fresh fruits and vegetables. Second, "processed food items" derived from the covered commodities are exempt, and USDA, in its final rule, defined this term broadly (at 7 C.F.R. §65.220). Essentially, any time a covered commodity is subjected to a change that alters its basic character, it is considered to be processed. Although adding salt, water, or sugar do not, under USDA's definition, change the basic character, virtually any sort of cooking, curing, or mixing apparently does. For example, roasting a peanut or pecan, mixing peas with carrots, or breading a piece of meat or chicken all count as processing. As a result, only about 30% of the U.S. beef supply, 11% of all pork, 39% of chicken, and 40% of all fruit and vegetable supplies may be covered by COOL requirements at the retail level.[12] Whole peanuts are almost always purchased in roasted form, and will not have to be labeled. Some critics argued that AMS overstepped its authority, and congressional intent, by excepting such minimally processed commodities.

AMS countered that in fact many imported items still must carry COOL under provisions of the Tariff Act of 1930. "For example, while a bag of frozen peas and carrots is considered a processed food item under the COOL final rule, if the peas and carrots are of foreign origin, the Tariff Act requires that the country of origin be marked on the bag," AMS argued, citing similar regulatory situations for roasted nuts and for a variety of seafood items.[13]

Vilsack's letter, however, acknowledged that the "processed foods" definition in the final rule "may be too broadly drafted. Even if products are subject to curing, smoking, broiling, grilling, or steaming, voluntary labeling would be appropriate," he wrote.

Record-Keeping, Verification, and Penalties

The COOL law prohibits USDA from using a mandatory animal identification (ID) system,[14] but the original 2002 version stated that the Secretary "may require that any person that prepares, stores, handles, or distributes a covered commodity for retail sale maintain a verifiable record-keeping audit trail that will permit the Secretary to verify compliance." Verification immediately became one of the most contentious issues, particularly for livestock producers, in part because of the potential complications and costs to affected industries of tracking animals and their products from birth through retail sale. Producers of plant-based commodities, as well as food retailers and others, also expressed concern about the cost and difficulty of maintaining records for commodities that are highly fungible and often widely sourced. The 2008 law eased these requirements somewhat by stating that USDA "may conduct an audit of any person that prepares, stores, handles, or distributes a covered commodity" in order to verify compliance. Such persons must provide verification, but USDA may not ask for any additional records beyond those maintained "in the course of the normal conduct of business."

---

[12] Percentages calculated by CRS based on USDA estimates of retail-level COOL coverage in pounds, divided by total annual supply (USDA data on domestic production plus imports).

[13] AMS, "Frequently Asked Questions," January 12, 2009, available at http://www.ams.usda.gov/AMSv1.0/getfile?dDocName=STELPRDC5074846.

[14] For information on this related issue, see CRS Report R40832, *Animal Identification and Traceability Overview and Issues*, by Joel Greene.

In its final rule, AMS stated that covered persons generally would have to keep records for one year that can identify both the immediate previous source and the immediate subsequent recipient of a covered commodity; certain exceptions are provided for pre-labeled products. Also, a slaughter facility can accept a producer affidavit as sufficient evidence for animal origin claims.

Also, potential fines for willful noncompliance are set for retailers and other persons at no more than $1,000 per violation. The 2002 law had set the fine at no more than $10,000 (and for retailers only), but the 2008 farm bill lowered this amount.

Administrative Enforcement and Audits

USDA's Agricultural Marketing Service implements COOL through cooperative agreements with all 50 states.[15] During FY2010, state agencies conducted 8,363 retail surveillance reviews to ensure compliance with COOL requirements. These reviews involved the auditing of 200 products as they moved from initial suppliers to retail shelves. AMS resources (i.e., appropriated funding of almost $10.7 million and 14 staff years in FY2011) are available to train federal and state employees on enforcement responsibilities, conduct supply chain audits, analyze and respond to formal complaints, and develop educational and outreach activities for retailers, suppliers, and other interested parties. During FY2011, AMS planned to implement a real-time database to track the findings of federal-state retail reviews, enforcement actions taken, and other information viewed as critical to COOL operations.[16]

USDA's Office of Inspector General (OIG) audited the operations of the COOL program during 2010. Its report noted that "AMS made significant strides implementing the final rule" but found the need for improvements in its controls and processes to ensure that retailers and suppliers fully comply with COOL regulations." The OIG identified the need for AMS to strengthen its process to select retailers to be reviewed and the review process itself, and to more quickly evaluate the documentation kept by retailers and issue noncompliance letters. Auditors also pointed out that AMS needs to be more vigorous in enforcing COOL requirements, provide better oversight of the state agencies that conduct retailer reviews, and improve how it communicates with and provides program guidance to retailers. AMS agreed with all of the OIG recommendations, and has taken, or will take, steps to put them into effect.[17]

In reviews conducted in FY2009 and FY2010 in retail stores, AMS found that almost three-quarters of the findings of noncompliance with COOL were due to the lack of labeling on covered commodities. The second most frequent finding was that of inaccurate labeling (14%). Vegetables and fruit accounted for a much higher rate of not complying with COOL requirements than any other commodity group.[18]

---

[15] AMS maintains an extensive website on COOL, with links to implementing regulations, cost-benefit analysis, and other materials at http://www.ams.usda.gov/cool/.

[16] USDA, FY2012 Budget Explanatory Notes for Committee on Appropriations for Agricultural Marketing Service, pp. 19-5, 19-14 to 19-15, 19g-10, and 19-47, http://www.obpa.usda.gov/19ams2012notes.pdf.

[17] USDA, OIG, "Implementation of Country of Origin Labeling," August 2011, pp. 1 and 4, http://www.usda.gov/oig/webdocs/01601-04-HY.pdf.

[18] USDA, AMS, "COOL—Retail Compliance FY2009-2010," http://www.ams.usda.gov/AMSv1.0/getfile?dDocName=STELPRDC5093595.

COOL Challenged by Canada and Mexico in WTO

Canada and Mexico are major suppliers of live cattle and hogs that are fed in U.S. feeding facilities and/or processed into beef and pork in U.S. meat packing plants. As the U.S. meat processing sector geared up to implement COOL in mid-2008, Canada and Mexico expressed concern that COOL would adversely impact their livestock sectors. Indeed, U.S. cattle imports from Canada and Mexico and hog imports from Canada dropped in both 2008 and 2009 from year-earlier levels. Some analyses supported claims that COOL hampered livestock imports. Other analyses pointed out that factors such as exchange rates and inventory levels were also affecting import levels and that declines could not be entirely attributed to COOL (see **Appendix C** for background on livestock trade in North America).

Canada and Mexico requested consultations with the United States in December 2008 and June 2009 about their concerns. Not satisfied with the outcome of these consultations with U.S. officials, both countries in early October 2009 requested the establishment of a WTO dispute settlement (DS) panel to consider their case. In response, the U.S. Trade Representative (USTR) and the Secretary of Agriculture commented that they "regretted that the formal consultations" did not resolve concerns, and stated their belief that U.S. implementation of COOL provides consumers with information that is consistent with WTO commitments. They noted that countries worldwide had agreed that the principle of country-of-origin labeling was legitimate policy long before the WTO was created, and that other countries also require goods to be labeled with their origin.[19]

Both the Canadian and Mexican governments, in requesting a panel, asserted that COOL is inconsistent with U.S. obligations under certain WTO agreements—the General Agreement on Tariffs and Trade 1994, the Agreement on Technical Barriers to Trade, and the Agreement on Rules of Origin. These obligations include treating imports no less favorably than like products of domestic origin; making sure that product-related requirements are not more trade-restrictive than necessary to fulfill a legitimate public policy objective; ensuring that compliance with laws on marks of origin does not result in damaging imports, reducing their value, or unreasonably increasing their cost; and ensuring that laws, rules, and procedures on country of origin do not "themselves create restrictive, distorting, or disruptive" international trade, among others.

On November 19, 2009, the WTO's Dispute Settlement Body established a panel to consider both countries' complaints. In proceeding with this WTO case, Canadian officials stated that the COOL requirements are "so onerous" that when they were implemented, Canadian exporters of cattle and hogs were discriminated against in the U.S. market. The Canadian beef and pork industries, led by the Canadian Cattlemen's Association (CCA) and the Canadian Pork Council, actively pushed their government to initiate a WTO challenge. The CCA argued that COOL cost its producers C$92 million over the two months following the publication of the interim rule in August 2008, and could cost C$500 million per year. CCA estimated that slaughter steers and heifers were losing C$90 per head, because U.S. meat establishments did not want to assume the increased costs of complying with new labeling requirements by segregating, holding, and then slaughtering Canadian cattle separately from U.S. cattle. The losses included lower prices for all Canadian cattle due to decreased U.S. demand, as well as the cost of shipping those that are sold

---

[19] U.S. Trade Representative, "Vilsack, Kirk Comment on Canadian Panel Request Regarding Country-of-Origin Labeling," October 7, 2009, http://www.ustr.gov/about-us/press-office/press-releases/2009/october/vilsack-kirk-comment-canadian-panel-request-regard.

further distances to the fewer number of U.S. plants willing to take them. Canadian pork producers expressed similar concerns.[20]

USTR's request for public comment on this pending WTO case generated responses that reflected the heated debate on mandatory COOL seen earlier among key players in the livestock sector. The American Meat Institute (AMI), representing U.S. meat processors and packers, stated that the U.S. law, in addition to violating WTO commitments, also violates NAFTA commitments. AMI argued that COOL discriminates against imports in favor of domestic meat.[21]

In opposition, the U.S. Cattlemen's Association (USCA) and the National Farmers Union argued that COOL is "fully consistent" with the General Agreement on Tariffs and Trade and the Agreement on Technical Barriers to Trade (key WTO commitments). Both stated that COOL "does not discriminate between domestic and imported beef ... [and] operates neutrally in the market place," and noted that COOL does not impose any domestic content requirements (i.e., does not stipulate what share of value or quantity determines country of origin).[22] The Ranchers-Cattlemen Action Legal Fund, United Stockgrowers of America (R-CALF USA), presented similar comments.[23]

The National Cattlemen's Beef Association (NCBA) expressed concern that Canada's decision to pursue its case against U.S. COOL rules has the potential for retaliatory action to be taken against U.S. beef. It noted that "COOL has damaged critically important trading relationships [i.e., the import of Canadian and Mexican livestock, the value added as they pass through U.S. feedlots and are processed into meat, and the export of finished meat products back to Mexican and Canadian consumers], and is not putting additional money into the pockets of cattlemen."[24]

Dispute Panel Ruling

On November 18, 2011, the WTO DS panel ruled that certain COOL requirements violate two articles of the WTO Agreement on Technical Barriers to Trade (TBT) and the requirement for impartial administration of regulations laid out in the General Agreement on Tariffs and Trade 1994 (GATT 1994).[25] The panel concluded that the COOL "measure"—the statute and the final rule—constituted a "technical regulation" under the TBT Agreement and was thus subject to TBT obligations. It further found that the COOL measure (1) treated imported livestock less favorably than "like domestic livestock," particularly in the labeling of muscle cut meats (beef and pork), in violation of the national treatment obligation in the TBT's Article 2.1; and (2) failed to meet the

---

[20] Various trade publication reports, including *Cattle Buyers Weekly,* "MCOOL Has Cost Canadian Producers C$92M," December 8, 2008; *Agri-Pulse,* "COOL Regulations Create Heartburn for Canadians," December 3, 2008; and *Washington Trade Daily,* December 2, 2008, pp. 3-4.

[21] AMI, "American Meat Institute Tells U.S. Trade Representative That Mandatory Country-of-Origin Labeling Violates International Trade Obligations," January 8, 2010, http://www.meatami.com/ht/display/ReleaseDetails/i/56358.

[22] USCA, "USCA and Farmers Union Urge Vigorous COOL Defense," January 12, 2010, http://www.uscattlemen.org/TheNewsRoom/2010_News/1-12COOLdefense.htm.

[23] R-CALF USA, "Canada, Mexico Have No Standing to Bring Complaint Against U.S. COOL Law," July 2, 2009, http://www.r-calfusa.com/news_releases/2009/090702-canada htm.

[24] NCBA, "NCBA Statement on Canadian WTO Complaint against U.S. COOL Law," October 7, 2009, http://www.beefusa.org/NEWSNCBAStatementonCanadianWTOComplaintagainstUSCOOLLaw39616.aspx.

[25] CRS Legislative Attorneys Emily Barbour and Jeanne Grimmett contributed to this section summarizing the panel's ruling.

---

legitimate objective of providing information to consumers on the origin of meat products, and thus violated the TBT's Article 2.2. The panel also found that the Vilsack letter's "suggestions for voluntary action" went beyond COOL's obligations and, while not a "technical regulation," constitute unreasonable administration of COOL itself, thus violating Article X:3(a) of the GATT 1994.[26] The panel concluded that the United States has "nullified or impaired benefits" to which Canada and Mexico are entitled, and recommended that the WTO's Dispute Settlement Body (DSB)[27] request the United States to conform these "inconsistent measures" with its obligations under the TBT Agreement and GATT 1994.[28] These three findings, along with the subsequent decisions made by the WTO Appellate Body on two findings appealed by the United States, are discussed below.

U.S. Appeal of the WTO Panel Ruling

Under WTO rules, the United States had various options available to respond to the dispute panel's adverse ruling on certain aspects of U.S. COOL. One was to accept the decision and make changes to the COOL statute and/or regulations to comply with the WTO findings. Another was to appeal the panel report on legal issues.[29]

On March 23, 2012, the United States appealed the WTO DS panel's report to the WTO Appellate Body (AB).[30] The USTR spokeswoman restated USTR's position that the report had confirmed the U.S. right to adopt rules to inform consumers of the country of origin in their purchasing decisions, but expressed disappointment that the panel "disagreed with the way that the United States designed its COOL requirements" for beef and pork. USTR's chief counsel stated that the U.S. appeal is "a signal of our commitment" to ensure that consumers "are provided with accurate and relevant information" on the origin of beef and pork, and "to fight for the interests of U.S. consumers at the WTO."[31] On June 29, 2012, the WTO's AB upheld the DS panel's finding that the COOL measure treats imported Canadian cattle and hogs, and imported Mexican cattle, less favorably than like domestic livestock, due to its record-keeping and verification requirements. The AB, however, reversed the panel's finding that COOL does not fulfill its legitimate objective

---

[26] The TBT Agreement is summarized in CRS Report R41306, *Trade Law An Introduction to Selected International Agreements and U.S. Laws*, by Jeanne J. Grimmett. The GATT 1994 commitment refers to the provision that requires laws and regulations to be administered "in a uniform, impartial and reasonable manner."

[27] The Dispute Settlement Body has the sole authority to establish "panels" of experts to consider a trade dispute case filed by any WTO member country, and to accept or reject the panels' findings or the results of an appeal. It monitors the implementation of the rulings and recommendations, and has the power to authorize retaliation when a country does not comply with a ruling.

[28] WTO, *United States—Certain Country of Origin Labelling (COOL) Requirements*, Reports of the Panel, WT/DS384/R, WT/DS386/R, November 18, 2011, http://www.wto.org/english/tratop_e/dispu_e/384_386r_e.pdf. Background on the COOL dispute case is available on the WTO's website at http://wto.org/english/tratop_e/dispu_e/ cases_e/ds384_e.htm (Canada) and http://wto.org/english/tratop_e/dispu_e/cases_e/ds386_e.htm (Mexico).

[29] CRS Legislative Attorney Jeanne Grimmett contributed to the sections summarizing the WTO's appeals process for panel reports and the WTO procedures that would apply if the United States is not successful with its appeal.

[30] This "is a standing body of seven persons that hears appeals from reports issued by panels in disputes brought by WTO Members. ... Appellate Body Reports, once adopted by the Dispute Settlement Body (DSB), must be accepted by the parties to the dispute." See http://wto.org/english/tratop_e/dispu_e/appellate_body_e.htm.

[31] Reuters, "U.S. to appeal WTO ruling against meat labels," March 23, 2012 (hereinafter cited as Reuters); Agri-Pulse.com, "USTR will appeal WTO ruling on COOL," March 23, 2012. USTR's appeal submission to the WTO is available at http://www.ustr.gov/sites/default/files/US.AppellantSub.fin_.pdf.

---

to provide consumers with information on origin. These determinations are briefly highlighted in "WTO Findings," below.

WTO Findings

COOL Treats Imported Livestock Less Favorably than Domestic Livestock

The DS panel found that Canada and Mexico demonstrated that COOL is a technical regulation governed by, and in violation of, Article 2.1 of the TBT. The AB upheld this finding, but for different reasons (see below). This TBT article states: "Members shall ensure that in respect of technical regulations, products imported from the territory of any Member shall be accorded treatment no less favourable than that accorded to like products of national origin and to like products originating in any other country." The panel first found that the COOL statute and the final rule (but not the Vilsack letter) are a "technical regulation" because they are legally enforceable requirements governing the labeling of meat products offered for sale.[32] The panel further found that Canadian and U.S. cattle, Canadian and U.S. hogs, and Mexican and U.S. cattle are "like products," and the muscle cut labels used to implement COOL affect competitive conditions for these products in the U.S. market to the detriment of imported livestock. According to the panel, COOL creates this "competitive advantage" by creating an incentive for "processing exclusively domestic livestock and a disincentive against handling imported livestock." More specifically, the panel found that to comply with COOL, processors need to segregate imported from domestic livestock to an extent that discourages them from using imported livestock at all. In turn, this reduces the competitive opportunities for imported livestock relative to those for domestic livestock. This is the first time that a WTO dispute panel took trade effects into account in determining whether "less favorable treatment" was accorded to like products under Article 2.1.

The panel based this conclusion on its assessment of the compliance requirements of COOL. It first reviewed the four statutory definitions used to label the origin of beef and pork muscle cuts (**Table 1**), noting that "origin is determined by the country in which specific livestock production and processing steps took place (i.e., birth, raising and slaughtering)," and highlighted the distinctions between the exclusive U.S. origin label and the other three labels that identified livestock with an imported element (i.e., at least one step took place outside the United States). It observed that "there was ... major flexibility" under COOL's interim final rule (August 2008) to use "multiple countries of origin" (Category B) for muscle cuts eligible for the U.S.-origin only label (Category A) "without limitations." However, as a response to public comment, COOL's final rule (January 2009) ended this flexibility, allowing the multiple countries declaration (Category B) to be used to label U.S.-origin meat only if U.S. and foreign livestock were commingled for slaughter "on a single production day."

---

[32] The panel made its determination on what is, and is not, a technical regulation with reference to TBT's Annex 1.1. It defines such to be a document that spells out "labeling requirements" among other features, including administrative provisions, "with which compliance is mandatory." The panel concluded that the COOL statute and final rule are "legal instruments that are legally binding in US law," with wording clearly mandating compliance, while the Vilsack letter, rather than mandating additional labeling requirements, presents them as "suggestions for voluntary action."

Table 1. COOL for Beef and Pork: From Statute to Label

Muscle Cuts & Ground Meat Categories	COOL Statutory Definition	AMS Final Rule (January 2009)	COOL Label at Retail Level
UNITED STATES COUNTRY OF ORIGIN [Category A]	"beef [or] ... pork ... derived from an animal that was ... exclusively born, raised, and slaughtered in the United States"	For beef and pork, means: "(1) From animals *exclusively born, raised, and slaughtered in the United States*; (2) From animals born and raised in Alaska or Hawaii and transported for a period of not more than 60 days through Canada to the United States and slaughtered in the United States; ..."	Product of the US(A)
MULTIPLE COUNTRIES OF ORIGIN [Category B]	"beef [or] ... pork ... derived from an animal that is— (i) not exclusively born, raised and slaughtered in the United States; (ii) born, raised or slaughtered in the United States; and (iii) not imported into the United States for immediate slaughter"	For muscle cuts of beef and pork "derived from animals that were *born in Country X or (as applicable) Country Y, raised and slaughtered in the United States*, and were *not derived from animals imported for immediate slaughter* [defined as "consignment directly from the port of entry to a recognized slaughtering establishment and slaughtered within 2 weeks from the date of entry"], the origin may be designated as Product of the United States, Country X, and (as applicable) Country Y." For muscle cuts of beef and pork "derived from animals *born, raised, and slaughtered in the U.S.* that are *commingled during a production day* with muscle cuts [of beef and pork from animals *born outside the U.S., raised and slaughtered in the U.S., and not imported for immediate slaughter*], the origin may be designated as Product of the United States, Country X, and (as applicable) Country Y." For muscle cuts of beef and pork "derived from animals that are *born in Country X or Country Y, raised and slaughtered in the United States*, that are *commingled during a production day with muscle cut*[s of beef and pork] *derived from animals that are imported into the United States for immediate slaughter* ..., the origin may be designated as Product of the United States, Country X, and (as applicable) Country Y." "In each case, the countries may be listed in any order. In addition, the origin declaration may include more specific information related to production steps provided records to substantiate the claims are maintained and the claim is consistent with other app icable Federal legal requirements."	Product of the US, Country X, and Country Y (if app icable)
IMPORTED FOR IMMEDIATE SLAUGHTER [Category C]	"beef [or] ... pork ... derived from an animal that is imported into the United States for immediate slaughter"	"If an animal was imported into the United States *for immediate slaughter* [defined as "consignment directly from the port of entry to a recognized slaughtering establishment and slaughtered within 2 weeks from the date of entry"], the origin of the resulting [beef and pork] derived from that animal shall be designated as Product of Country X and the United States."	Product of Country X, US
FOREIGN COUNTRY OF ORIGIN [Category D]	"beef [or] ... pork ... derived from an animal ... not born, raised, or slaughtered in the United States"	"Imported [beef and pork] for which origin has already been established as defined by this law (e.g., born, raised, and slaughtered or produced) and for which *no production steps have occurred in the United States*, shall retain their origin, as declared to U.S. Customs and Border Protection at the time the product entered the United States, through retail sale."	Product of Country X

Muscle Cuts & Ground Meat Categories	COOL Statutory Definition	AMS Final Rule (January 2009)	COOL Label at Retail Level
GROUND BEEF OR PORK	"notice ... for ground beef, ground pork ... shall include a list of all [or] ... all reasonably possible countries of origin of such ground beef, ground pork, ..."	"The declaration for ground beef, ground pork, ... shall *list all countries of origin contained therein or that may be reasonably contained* therein. In determining what is considered reasonable, when a raw material from a specific origin is not in a processor's inventory for more than 60 days, that country shall no longer be included as a possible country of origin."	Product of US, Country X, [and as app icable] Country Y, Country Z, ...

Source: 7 U.S.C. §§1638a(a)(2)(A)-(D), Section 282 of Agricultural Marketing Act of 1946, as amended by 2008 farm bill (§10816 of P.L. 107-171); 7 CFR 65.260(a)(1), 65.300(e)(1)-(4) and 65.300(h), as published in the *Federal Register,* January 15, 2008, p. 2706; Agricultural Marketing Service, "Labeling Options," p. 2, http://www.ams.usda.gov/AMSv1.0/getfile?dDocName=STELPRDC5074845.

Notes: Key terms are in italics. These same designations also apply to other covered meats (lamb, chicken, and goat meat), but they were not the subject of complaints filed by Canada and Mexico in the WTO case.

The panel then examined what is involved in segregating livestock and meat between domestic and foreign origin under five business scenarios. It determined that "the least costly way" to comply with COOL "is to rely on exclusively domestic livestock" rather than imported livestock. Accepting evidence provided by Canada and Mexico that major U.S. slaughterhouses are "applying a considerable COOL discount of [US$] 40-60 per head for imported livestock" but not to domestic livestock, the panel observed that COOL creates an incentive to process domestic rather than imported livestock because it is less costly to do so. It pointed out that several U.S. meat processors indicated they plan to move to use Category A (U.S. origin) "for the vast majority of their beef and pork products" and to ensure segregation by origin (i.e., minimize commingling). Other evidence presented confirmed that the U.S.-origin label accounts for a large share of the meat marketed. The United States indicated that 71% of the beef, and 70% of the pork, sold at the retail level carries the exclusive U.S. label. Canada showed that close to 90% of meat sold at retail carries this U.S. label. Based on the above, the panel "preliminarily" concluded that COOL "creates an incentive to use domestic livestock—and a disincentive to handle imported livestock—by imposing higher segregation costs on imported livestock than on domestic livestock." The panel's report also showed that some U.S. plants and companies "are simply refusing to process any imported livestock any more," and that fewer U.S. processing plants are accepting cattle and hog imports than before. It also noted that certain suppliers had to transport imported livestock longer distances than before COOL, and that they also faced logistical problems and additional costs for timing delivery to specific times or days when processing is scheduled. Although the panel took these into account, it decided it also was important to make findings on COOL's actual trade effects. To do this, it considered data, economic analyses, and econometric studies submitted by Canada, Mexico, and the United States.

In reviewing two economic studies on COOL's livestock segregation costs submitted by Canada, the panel stated "both studies shed some light on the different types of segregation and compliance costs encountered at different stages of the supply chain." Noting that such costs need to be absorbed somewhere in the marketing system, it concluded that "economic competition pressure" will dictate how these costs are allocated. Whether this involves processing only U.S.-origin livestock because it is the cheapest way to comply with COOL and because many U.S. consumers are not willing to pay a price premium for country-of-origin labeling, or incurring the additional costs associated with segregating imported livestock before processing, either option "is likely to cause a decrease in the volume and price of imported livestock."

The panel also reviewed econometric analyses[33] submitted by Canada and the United States that purported to assess COOL's impacts on prices and shares of imported livestock. Whereas the Canadian study concluded that COOL caused the reduced competitive opportunities for Canadian livestock in the U.S. market, the U.S. study concluded that the economic recession was the primary cause. Rather than seeking to reconcile these disparate conclusions, the panel instead assessed "the robustness of each study." It considered Canada's study to be "sufficiently robust" because it included other economic variables that confirmed that COOL—not the economic recession that began in 2008, the 2004-2005 U.S. import ban due to the discovery of BSE in Canada's cattle herds, or transport costs—"had a negative and significant impact on Canadian import shares and price basis." Conversely, the panel found the U.S. study did not sufficiently show that the economic recession rather than COOL accounted for the negative impacts experienced in the cattle sector, did not fully analyze what occurred in both countries' hog sectors, and thus did not refute what Canada's study laid out.

In reviewing the U.S. appeal of this finding, the Appellate Body found that the panel's analysis was incomplete in not considering whether or not the detrimental impact on imports were due exclusively to a "legitimate regulatory distinction." The AB found that the COOL measure

> lacks even-handedness because its recordkeeping and verification requirements impose a disproportionate burden on upstream producers and processors of livestock as compared to the information conveyed to consumers through the mandatory labelling requirements for meat sold at the retail level. That is, although a large amount of information must be tracked and transmitted by upstream producers for purposes of providing consumers with information on origin, only a small amount of this information is actually communicated to consumers in an understandable or accurate manner, including because a considerable proportion of meat sold in the United States is not subject to the COOL measure's labelling requirements at all.[34]

Because the detrimental impacts did not have a sufficient regulatory basis, the AB found the measure to be discriminatory against imports and thus upheld the DS panel's finding.

Ground Meat Label Does Not Result in Less Favorable Treatment for Imported Livestock

The DS panel determined that, unlike the muscle cut labels, the ground meat labels were consistent with Article 2.1 of the TBT. It found that the 60-day "inventory allowance" gives significant flexibility to processors (e.g., beef grinders) in labeling country of origin. This rule is based on the statutory requirement that ground meat labels list all actual or "reasonably possible" countries of origin. In practice, the rule allows a processor to use the same label for all of its ground meat so long as the label lists all countries of origin of the meat in the processor's inventory for the last 60 days. Moreover, the 60-day "inventory allowance" flexibility is available not only for meat processors, but for market participants at every stage of meat supply and distribution. The panel determined that, contrary to Canada and Mexico's assertions, the rule's

---

[33] These involve applying mathematics and statistical methods to study relationships between economic variables.

[34] WTO, United States—Certain Country of Origin Labelling (COOL) Requirements, 'Summary of key findings," available at http://www.wto.org/english/tratop_e/dispu_e/cases_e/ds384_e.htm.

flexibility "limits any additional costs of implementing" the ground meat labeling requirements. Canada and Mexico did not present any evidence that, *despite* this flexibility, compliance with COOL for ground meat affected imported livestock less favorably than domestic livestock. Canada and Mexico did not appeal this finding to the AB.

COOL Does Not Meet Objective of Providing Consumers with Information on Origin of Meats

Canada and Mexico also alleged that COOL violates Article 2.2 of the TBT by being more trade-restrictive than necessary to fulfill a legitimate policy objective. Article 2.2 reads: "Members shall ensure that technical regulations are not prepared, adopted or applied with a view to or with the effect of creating unnecessary obstacles to international trade. For this purpose, technical regulations *shall not be more trade-restrictive than necessary to fulfil a legitimate objective*, taking account of the risks non-fulfillment would create. Such legitimate objectives are, *inter alia*: national security requirements; the prevention of deceptive practices; protection of human health or safety, animal or plant life or health, or the environment. In assessing such risks, relevant elements of consideration are, *inter alia*: available scientific and technical information, related processing technology or intended end-uses of products" (italics added for emphasis). The panel accepted the U.S. position that COOL's objective is to inform consumers of the country of origin of meat products,[35] and it agreed with the United States that this is a "legitimate" policy objective under TBT's Article 2.2 to pursue. However, it concluded that COOL's implementation is more trade-restrictive than necessary to fulfill this objective because it does not, in fact, meaningfully inform consumers about the countries of origin of meat products. In other words, the panel held that because COOL is both trade-restrictive by virtue of its inconsistency with Article 2.1 of the TBT and ineffective at achieving its policy objective, it is "more trade-restrictive than necessary."

In reaching its conclusion that COOL does not achieve its objective, the DS panel agreed with Canada and Mexico that the labels identifying multiple countries of origin could confuse or mislead, rather than inform, consumers. It noted that a consumer could not readily distinguish the origins of meat products listed on a Category B label as coming from multiple countries, from the origins of meat products shown on a Category C label as coming from those same multiple countries (e.g., Product of the United States, Canada [Category B], compared to Product of Canada, United States [Category C]) (**Table 1**). The panel added that because processors have the flexibility to use both types of labels interchangeably for commingled meat (i.e., meat processed from animals of different origins), the labels not only fail to inform the average consumer of the distinction between them but could also mislead a fully informed consumer about the precise origins of some meat products.

However, the Appellate Body found that the DS panel erred in interpreting and applying Article 2.2. Although it agreed with the panel that COOL's objective is to provide consumers with information on origin and that this is a legitimate objective, the AB viewed the panel's finding as too narrow. Its summary states that the panel "ignored its own findings, which demonstrated that the COOL measure does contribute, at least to some extent, to achieving its objective." The AB

---

[35] The panel rejected Canada's and Mexico's argument that COOL's objective is to protect the domestic U.S. livestock industry (p. 143 of WTO panel's report; see footnote 28).

reversed the panel's finding, but was not able to determine whether COOL is more trade-restrictive than necessary to meet the TBT requirement that it be a legitimate objective.[36]

Vilsack Letter Is Not a Technical Regulation

Although the panel recognized that the Vilsack letter was not a technical regulation within the scope of the TBT Agreement, the panel agreed with Canada and Mexico that the Vilsack letter violates Article X:3(a) of GATT 1994 (see "Vilsack Letter," above, for details). This article states that "[e]ach contracting party shall administer in a uniform, impartial and reasonable manner all its laws, regulations, decisions and rulings ..." Specifically, the panel found that the letter is an unreasonable act of administering COOL because (1) it could not find any "justifiable rationale" for simultaneously permitting the final rule to enter into force and suggesting stricter practices than the ones the rule requires, (2) the language of the letter may have caused uncertainty and confusion as to its force and effect, and (3) its timing relative to the final rule's entry into force may have caused confusion about whether processors should comply with the final rule or the Vilsack letter. The letter, it wrote, did not meet the minimum standards for transparency and procedural fairness in the administration of trade regulations. In its appeal, Canada requested that the AB make certain rulings on the Vilsack letter, but this was withdrawn after the United States asserted that this measure had been withdrawn.

Reaction to WTO DS Panel and Appellate Body Reports

United States

With the WTO's release of the DS panel's report, USTR welcomed its affirmation of "the right of the United States to require country of origin labeling for meat products." Acknowledging that the panel disagreed with the details on how the U.S. COOL requirements were designed, it expressed the U.S. commitment to provide "consumers with accurate and relevant information [on] the origin of meat products that they buy at the retail level." USTR stated that it would consider all options going forward, including an appeal.[37]

The U.S. meat sector expressed mixed reactions. Those in favor of making changes to COOL to address the panel's conclusions include the National Cattlemen's Beef Association (NCBA), the National Pork Producers Council (NPPC), and the American Meat Institute (AMI). The NCBA advised against appealing this ruling. Instead, it urged USTR to work "to apply pressure on Congress to bring the United States into WTO compliance across the board" and to act quickly before Canada and Mexico—two important trading partners—impose "unnecessary and unfortunate tariffs" on U.S. agricultural exports. The NPPC "will be working with lawmakers to craft a legislative fix so that [COOL] is WTO-compliant" to avoid risking "retaliation from and a trade war with Canada and Mexico." AMI commented that the ruling "was not surprising," stating that it had "contended for years ... that [COOL] was not just costly and cumbersome, but a violation of our country's WTO obligations."[38]

---

[36] WTO, United States—Certain Country of Origin Labelling (COOL) Requirements, 'Summary of key findings," available at http://www.wto.org/english/tratop_e/dispu_e/cases_e/ds384_e.htm.

[37] USTR, "Statement in Response to WTO Panel Decision on Country of Origin Labeling," November 18, 2011, http://www.ustr.gov/about-us/press-office/press-releases/2011/november/statement-office-us-trade-representative-response.

[38] NCBA, "Statement ... [on] WTO Ruling on US Country of Origin Labeling," http://www.beefusa.org/ (continued...)

Livestock groups that support COOL as now implemented include the Ranchers-Cattlemen Action Legal Fund (R-CALF) and the U.S. Cattlemen's Association (USCA). R-CALF responded that "the WTO is trying to usurp our nation's sovereignty," questioning "when do we allow an international tribunal to dictate to our U.S. Congress what is or is not a legitimate objective of providing information to United States' citizens?" The USCA strongly disagreed with the panel's findings, but was pleased that the report "affirmed the right of the U.S. to label meat for consumers." Its president expressed support for USTR's efforts to defend U.S. rights, pledging to assist "with the appeal process" and to work "with our allies in the Administration and Congress to ensure that COOL continues."[39]

Other groups that had participated in the debate leading up to COOL's enactment also weighed in. The Food Marketing Institute (FMI) agreed with the panel's conclusion that COOL "fails to provide information in a meaningful way" and highlighted that "COOL enforcement has become more burdensome than ever ... for retailers." Its spokesman stated that COOL "will need to be repealed or rewritten for the U.S. to meet its [trade obligations]" and that FMI will work with Congress and USDA "to develop an alternative system" that informs consumers with useful information.[40] Among those supporting COOL, the National Farmers Union (NFU) responded that it will work with USTR and USDA "to ensure that COOL is implemented to the fullest extent of the law and in accordance with WTO." Its statement concluded that "if these results are unsatisfactory, then NFU will push to appeal the decision and continue to fight ... to ensure COOL is allowed to continue for as long as it takes to get this done." Public Citizen commented that the WTO's ruling against COOL for meats "make[s] it increasingly clear to the public that the WTO is leading a race to the bottom in consumer protection" by its second-guessing "the U.S. Congress, courts and public by elevating the goal of maximizing trade flows over consumer and environmental protection." Food and Water Watch urged the Administration to appeal the ruling, noting that the WTO "should not get to decide what U.S. consumers get to know about their food and should not be able to undermine rules put in place by U.S. elected officials."[41]

Members of Congress also hold diverse views on COOL's future. Some did not expect the WTO panel's decision on COOL to be favorable and view more "unwinnable" WTO cases as not in the "best interest" of U.S. agricultural producers. Senator Pat Roberts, ranking Member of the Senate Agriculture Committee, at a regional livestock meeting stated that he does not know of any market study that "shows American consumers will buy more American products with labels in

---

(...continued)

newsreleases1.aspx?NewsID=1248; *Pork Magazine*, "NPPC: What's on Tap for 2012?", January 2012, http://www.porknetwork.com/pork/pork-exec/Whats-on-Tap-for-2012-136695033.html; AMI, "WTO Rules in Favor of Canada in Complaint Over U.S. Country-of-Origin Labeling Law," http://www.meatami.com/ht/display/ArticleDetails/i/73951.

[39] R-CALF, "U.S. Sovereignty Usurped by WTO's COOL Decision," http://www.r-calfusa.com/news_releases/2011/111118-sovereignty.htm; USCA, "WTO Dispute Panel Issues Final COOL Report," http://www.uscattlemen.org/TheNewsRoom/2011_News/11-21WTO_DisputePanel.htm.

[40] FMI, "Food Retail Industry Applauds WTO Ruling on COOL," http://www.fmi.org/news_releases/index.cfm?fuseaction=mediatext&id=1277.

[41] NFU, "NFU Will Work With Administration to Ensure COOL Compliance With WTO Rules," http://nfu.org/news/65-international-policy/723-nfu-will-work-with-administration-to-ensure-cool-compliance-with-wto-rules; Public Citizen, "WTO Rules Against Country-of-Origin Meat Labeling Law: Third Ruling Against U.S. Consumer Safeguards in 2011", November 18, 2011, http://www.citizen.org/documents/release-wto-rules-against-coo-11-18-11.pdf; Food and Water Watch, "WTO Decision on COOL Attacks Consumers' Right to Know," November 18, 2011, http://www.foodandwaterwatch.org/pressreleases/wto-decision-on-cool-attacks-consumers%e2%80%99-right-to-know/

---

the store" and hoped "we can change people's minds."[42] By contrast, 19 Senators requested that the Obama Administration appeal the panel's ruling and "work to ensure that our COOL program both meets our international trade obligations while continuing to provide such information to consumers." Their letter expressed concern about the ruling's impact "on our ability to continue providing [COOL] information to consumers" and noted that congressional intent behind the 2008 statutory changes was for "such labeling [to] be nondiscriminatory in its treatment of imported products by requiring the labeling of both domestic as well as imported products." The letter further stated that the final COOL rule "appropriately establishes a labeling system which provides important and useful information to consumers while not placing an undue burden on the industry" and which "continues to provide the same opportunity for imported livestock to compete in the domestic marketplace as was the case prior to USDA's implementation of COOL."[43]

Canada

The Canadian government welcomed the panel's ruling as a "clear victory for Canada's livestock industry." Its Minister of Agriculture stated that the WTO decision "recognizes the integrated nature of the North American supply chain in this vitally important industry" and that "[r]emoving onerous labelling measures and unfair, unnecessary costs will improve competitiveness, boost growth and help strengthen the prosperity of Canadian and American producers alike." He expressed the hope this ruling "will open the door to a negotiated settlement of the dispute" and stressed Canada's commitment to work with the United States to "create a stronger more profitable livestock industry on both sides of the 49th parallel."[44]

The Canadian Pork Council (CPC) stated that the panel's report "vindicates [the] objections" the pork industry had to COOL legislation, which it believes restricts market access (i.e., the movement of live swine to the U.S. market) and constitutes a technical barrier. The CPC plans to work "with like-minded groups in the U.S. to find a meaningful solution without further litigation" (referring to a possible U.S. appeal and the process that would follow). The Canadian Cattlemen's Association (CCA) stated the ruling confirms Canada's position that COOL discriminates against live cattle shipped to the United States to the detriment of Canadian cattle producers. In particular, it noted that since taking effect, COOL "has increased costs for U.S. companies that import live Canadian cattle," which has reduced "the competiveness of those Canadian cattle in the U.S. market." The CCA plans to continue working with the U.S. industry "not ... for the outright repeal of COOL but [to] seek only those regulatory and statutory changes necessary to eliminate the discrimination that COOL has imposed to the comparative disadvantage of livestock imported into the U.S. vis-a-vis U.S. livestock."[45]

---

[42] *High Plains/Midwest Ag Journal*, "TCFA Members Face Scary Issues from Washington," November 14, 2011, http://www.hpj.com/archives/2011/nov11/nov14/1109TexasCattleFeedersjmlsr.cfm.

[43] Office of Senator Tim Johnson, "Johnson, Enzi to Administration: Keep COOL Strong," December 15, 2011, press release with text of letter, http://johnson.senate.gov/public/index.cfm?p=PressReleases.

[44] Foreign Affairs and International Trade Canada, "Canada Wins World Trade Organization Case on U.S. Country-of-Origin Labelling," November 18, 2011, http://www.international.gc.ca/media_commerce/comm/news-communiques/2011/349.aspx?lang=eng&view=d; Farmscape, "Canada Hopes for Negotiated Resolution of M-COOL Dispute," November 22, 2011, http://www.farmscape.com/f2ShowScript.aspx?i=23812&q=Canada+Hopes+for+Negotiated+Resolution+of+M-COOL+Dispute.

[45] CPC, "Canadian Pork Producers Welcome the WTO Panel Decision on COOL," November 18, 2011, http://www.cpc-ccp.com/documents/news-releases/FINALWTOpaneldecisionpressrelease.pdf; CCA, "WTO Rules Strongly in Favor of Canada in COOL Case," November 18, 2011, http://www.cattle.ca/media/file/original/ (continued...)

Reactions to the USTR Decision to Appeal

Interest groups that had urged the Obama Administration to appeal the WTO report (R-CALF, NCA, NFU, Food and Water Watch, Public Citizen) supported this decision.[46] Those that advocated resolving this dispute (NCBA, NPPC) expressed disappointment, and noted that the appeal jeopardizes strong trading relationships with Canada and Mexico and invites the prospect of retaliation by these two countries against U.S. meat exports.[47] (For background on all of these groups' positions, see "Reaction to WTO Panel Ruling, United States," above.)

Canada's Agriculture Minister expressed disappointment that the United States appealed, stating his confidence that the WTO findings "will be upheld so that trade can move more freely, benefiting producers and processors on both sides of the border." Mexico's Economic Ministry declared that it would defend Mexico's interests in the appeal process, and that it plans to file its own notice of appeal seeking a review of some issues in the panel's report that it says reflect inadequate legal analysis.[48]

Next Steps

Compliance under WTO Procedures with Appellate Body's Report

The Dispute Settlement Body will meet on July 10, 2012 to adopt the appellate report and the panel report, as modified by the AB, under the reverse consensus rule.[49] Under this rule, both reports will be adopted unless all WTO member countries present at the meeting vote not to do so. This rule makes adoption virtually automatic.[50] In turn, the United States, Canada, and Mexico will have to unconditionally accept the AB's decision.

(...continued)

1058_2011_11_18_CCA_News_Release_WTO_rules_strongly_in_favor_of_Canada_in_COOL_case.pdf.

[46] "R-CALF USA Applauds U.S. Appeal of WTO's Adverse COOL Ruling," March 23, 2012, http://www.tradereform.org/2012/03/r-calf-usa-applauds-u-s-appeal-of-wtos-adverse-cool-ruling/#comment-163002; "USCA Appreciates USTR Support for U.S. Cattle Producers," March 26, 2012, http://www.uscattlemen.org/TheNewsRoom/2012_News/3-26USTRSupport.htm; "NFU Applauds USTR Decision to Appeal WTO Ruling on COOL," March 23, 2012, http://nfu.org/news/212-international-policy/947-nfu-applauds-ustr-decision-to-appeal-wto-ruling-on-cool-; Food & Water Watch, "President Obama Finally Stands Up for U.S. Farmers and Consumers: U.S. Appeals WTO Decision on COOL," March 23, 2012; "Public Citizen Applauds Obama Administration's Efforts to Defend Consumer Country of Origin Meat Labeling; Appeal of WTO Ruling Necessary First Step," March 23, 2012, http://citizen.typepad.com/eyesontrade/2012/03/public-citizen-applauds-obama-administrations-efforts-to-defend-consumer-country-of-origin-meat-labe.html.

[47] "NCBA Statement on USTR Appeal of WTO Ruling on Country of Origin Labeling," http://www.beefusa.org/newsreleases1.aspx?newsid=2419; NPPC, "Capital Update, For the Week Ending March 23, 2012," http://www.nppc.org/2012/03/for-the-week-ending-march-23-2012/; Pork Network, "Pork, beef producers fear retaliation from COOL appeal," March 26, 2012, http://www.porknetwork.com/pork-news/latest/Pork-beef-producers-fear-retaliation-from-COOL-appeal-144248155.html.

[48] Reuters; Secretaría de Economía, "México continuará la defensa legal en OMC del caso COOL," March 23, 2012, http://www.economia.gob.mx/eventos-noticias/sala-de-prensa/informacion-relevante/7646-boletin087-12.

[49] CRS Legislative Attorney Jeanne Grimmett contributed to this section summarizing the WTO procedures that apply to complying with an AB report if a country is not successful with an appeal of a DS panel's findings.

[50] For details, see "Adoption of Panel Reports/Appellate Review (Articles 16, 17, 20)" in CRS Report RS20088, *Dispute Settlement in the World Trade Organization (WTO) An Overview*, by Jeanne J. Grimmett.

With the DSB expected to adopt both reports, the United States will need to take steps to comply with the key findings in the AB's report. Given that the compliance phase has not yet begun, the United States has not indicated what course of action it will pursue. But the United States likely at some point will begin the process to engage with both countries to resolve the dispute in a way that is mutually acceptable to all of the parties.

U.S. Options and Timetable

With the United States having lost its appeal on one of the DS panel's findings, USTR may initiate consultations with Canada and Mexico to explore options on how to comply with the AB's decision. Possible options include modifying those COOL provisions highlighted in the panel's report, replacing them with others, or eliminating them altogether. Also, the Administration is expected to engage in discussions with Congress on how to proceed. Certain beef and pork groups, some farm organizations, and those in the meat industry that support changing COOL have indicated that they will offer their suggestions on how the United States should comply. Opponents of amending COOL will weigh in against making any changes.

USTR, in consultation with Congress, stakeholders, and Canada and Mexico, will need to ascertain whether regulatory changes would suffice or whether the COOL statute would need to be amended to secure sufficient flexibility to address the AB's finding that imported Canadian cattle and hogs, and imported Mexican cattle, are treated less favorably than like domestic livestock.

If regulatory changes are determined to be sufficiently adequate to comply with the AB's finding, USDA would need to revisit the final regulations issued in January 2009 to implement COOL for beef and pork. But if changes in the COOL statute are required, the debate that would follow undoubtedly would bring back into the open long-standing divergent views on COOL's efficacy and cost. Congressional activity would likely mirror this debate.

Once the DSB adopts the DS panel and AB reports, the United States has 30 days to announce its plans for implementing the final findings. If the United States is unable to comply immediately, the WTO's Dispute Settlement Understanding (DSU) allows for a "reasonable period of time" for this to occur. For example, the United States could negotiate with Canada and Mexico what that time frame might be, among other possibilities that are laid out in the DSU. If the disputing countries fail to agree on a compliance deadline, the time period may be arbitrated. Often, WTO members are given approximately one year from the date of adoption of the panel report to comply; in any event, compliance that requires legislative action would likely be a more time-consuming effort than if only administrative action was required.

If the United States were not to comply with the WTO decision within the established compliance period, Canada and Mexico could request the United States to negotiate a compensation agreement. If an agreement is not requested, or if it is requested but an agreement is not reached, Canada and Mexico may request authorization from WTO's DSB to retaliate. The retaliation request is to be made within 30 days after the compliance period ends. This can involve the suspension of concessions or obligations owed by Canada and Mexico to the United States under a WTO agreement. One permitted action could involve Canada and Mexico increasing tariffs on agricultural products imported from the United States.[51] The United States may object to the retaliation request, in which case it would be automatically sent to arbitration.

Further, if the United States does not comply or only partially complies with the WTO decision, Canada and Mexico may also request that a compliance panel investigate whether the United States has in fact adopted a compliance measure or whether any measure that it has adopted is consistent with the WTO decision. Because WTO dispute settlement rules do not provide a timetable in the event that a party requests both authorization to retaliate and a compliance panel, disputing parties often enter into so-called "sequencing" agreements that accommodate both procedures.

If the United States ultimately decides to comply, the deadline to do so under the procedures outlined above may not occur until mid- to late 2013. Prevailing parties also have agreed on occasion to extend the original deadline in a dispute if progress is being made toward compliance. Those opposed to a long compliance period fear that, if the United States does not change certain aspects of COOL, Canada and Mexico—two significant markets for U.S. beef and pork—might retaliate by imposing tariffs on these products that now enter freely. At the same time, WTO Members have agreed in the WTO Dispute Settlement Understanding that they will not suspend WTO concessions or other obligations as retaliatory measures in a particular dispute unless authorized by the WTO Dispute Settlement Body. If that were to occur, the United States could challenge any unauthorized retaliation in a separate WTO dispute settlement proceeding.

Legislation in the 112th Congress

Observers point out that the 2008 farm bill amendments to the initial COOL statute were intended to balance the concerns of both proponents and opponents and to settle the longstanding controversy over requiring COOL for meats and other covered commodities. However, the outcome of the WTO challenge initiated by Canada and Mexico is now expected to influence the dynamics of COOL debate in the 112th Congress and beyond. Some lawmakers agree with some industry groups' criticisms of mandatory COOL and could offer legislation to limit its scope and impacts. Others may propose to narrowly amend the COOL statute to change only what is determined as necessary to respond to the details of the WTO decision. Other lawmakers remain strongly supportive of COOL as enacted and will oppose any significant rollback. For example, 19 Senators sent a letter to the Administration in late 2011 highlighting the WTO panel's validation of the right of the United States to require country-of-origin labeling and affirming that Congress's intent in the 2008 farm bill was to provide consumers with information on the origin of foods.[52] Also, Representative DeLauro on the House floor offered an amendment to exempt COOL from the proposed requirement in H.R. 10 that a joint resolution of approval be enacted before any economically significant rule (i.e., one with a $100 million annual impact on the economy) could take effect. Another measure seeks to bring more commodities under the scope of mandatory country-of-origin labeling. S. 831 (introduced by Senator Franken) would extend COOL requirements to fluid milk, cheese, yogurt, ice cream, butter, and other dairy products.

---

[51] For details, see "Compliance Panels (Article 21.5)" and "Compensation and Suspension of Concessions (Article 22)" in CRS Report RS20088, *Dispute Settlement in the World Trade Organization (WTO) An Overview*, by Jeanne J. Grimmett.

[52] See footnote 43.

Appendix A. Other Laws with Food Labeling Provisions

The COOL provisions of the 2002 and 2008 farm bills[53] do not change the requirements of the Tariff Act or the food safety inspection statutes described below. Instead, they were incorporated into the Agricultural Marketing Act of 1946 (Sections 281-285).

Tariff Act

Under Section 304 of the Tariff Act of 1930, as amended (19 U.S.C. 1304), every imported item must be conspicuously and indelibly marked in English to indicate to the "ultimate purchaser" its country of origin. The U.S. Customs and Border Protection generally defines the "ultimate purchaser" as the last U.S. person to receive the article in the form in which it was imported. So, articles arriving at the U.S. border in retail-ready packages—including food products, such as a can of Danish ham, or a bottle of Italian olive oil—must carry such a mark. However, if the article is destined for a U.S. processor where it will undergo "substantial transformation," the processor is considered the ultimate purchaser. Over the years, numerous technical rulings by Customs have determined what is, or is not, considered "substantial transformation," depending upon the item in question.

The law has authorized exceptions to labeling requirements, including articles on a so-called "J List," named for Section 1304(a)(3)(J) of the statute. This empowered the Secretary of the Treasury to exempt classes of items that were "imported in substantial quantities during the five-year period immediately preceding January 1, 1937, and were not required during such period to be marked to indicate their origin." Among the items placed on the J List were specified agricultural products including "natural products, such as vegetables, fruits, nuts, berries, and live or dead animals, fish and birds; all the foregoing which are in their natural state or not advanced in any manner further than is necessary for their safe transportation."[54] Although J List items themselves have been exempt from the labeling requirements, Section 304 of the 1930 act has required that their "immediate container" (essentially, the box they came in) have country-of-origin labels. But, for example, when Mexican tomatoes or Chilean grapes were sold unpackaged at retail in a store bin, country labeling had not been required by the Tariff Act.

Meat and Poultry Products Inspection Acts

USDA's Food Safety and Inspection Service (FSIS) is required to ensure the safety and proper labeling of most meat and poultry products, including imports, under the Federal Meat Inspection Act, as amended (21 U.S.C. 601 *et seq.*), and the Poultry Products Inspection Act, as amended (21 U.S.C. 451 *et seq.*). Regulations issued under these laws have required that country of origin appear in English on immediate containers of all meat and poultry products entering the United States (9 C.F.R. 327.14 and 9 C.F.R. 381.205). Only plants in countries certified by USDA to

---

[53] P.L. 107-171, Section 10816, approved May 13, 2002, 111 Stat. 533; and P.L. 110-246, Section 11002, approved June 18, 2008, 122 Stat. 2113. The COOL provisions in the AMA of 1946 are codified at 7 U.S.C. 1638 – 1638d.

[54] The J list is published in 19 C.F.R. 134.33, available at http://edocket.access.gpo.gov/cfr_2008/aprqtr/19cfr134 33.htm.

have inspection systems equivalent to those of the United States are eligible to export products to the United States.

All individual, retail-ready packages of imported meat products (for example, canned hams or packages of salami) have had to carry such labeling. Imported bulk products, such as carcasses, carcass parts, or large containers of meat or poultry destined for U.S. plants for further processing also have had to bear country-of-origin marks. However, once these non-retail items have entered the country, the federal meat inspection law has deemed them to be domestic products. When they are further processed in a domestic, FSIS-inspected meat or poultry establishment—which has been considered the ultimate purchaser for purposes of country-of-origin labeling—FSIS no longer requires such labeling on either the new product or its container. FSIS has considered even minimal processing, such as cutting a larger piece of meat into smaller pieces or grinding it for hamburger, enough of a transformation so that country markings are no longer necessary.

Meat and poultry product imports must comply not only with the meat and poultry inspection laws and rules but also with Tariff Act labeling regulations. Because Customs generally requires that imports undergo more extensive changes (i.e., "substantial transformation") than required by USDA to avoid the need for labeling, a potential for conflict has existed between the two requirements.

Federal Food, Drug, and Cosmetic Act

Foods other than meat and poultry are regulated by the U.S. Department of Health and Human Services' Food and Drug Administration (FDA), primarily under the Federal Food, Drug, and Cosmetic Act (FFDCA; 21 U.S.C. 301 et seq.). This act does not expressly require COOL for foods. Section 403(e) of the FFDCA does regard a *packaged* food to be misbranded if it lacks a label containing the name and place of business of the manufacturer, packer, or distributor (among other ways a food can be misbranded). However, this name and place of business is not an indicator of the origin of the product itself.

Appendix B. Timeline of COOL

Table B-1. COOL Developments & WTO Dispute Settlement Case

May 13, 2002	COOL provisions are enacted in the 2002 farm bill to take effect on September 30, 2004 (P.L. 107-171, §10816).
October 30, 2003	Agricultural Marketing Service (AMS) publishes in the *Federal Register* the proposed rule on COOL. The comment period, initially to close December 29, 2003, is extended to February 27, 2004.
January 23, 2004	Implementation of COOL for covered commodities except fish and shellfish is delayed until September 30, 2006, per enactment of the FY2004 omnibus appropriations act (P.L. 108-199, Division A, §749).
October 5, 2004	AMS publishes in the *Federal Register* the interim final rule on COOL for fish and shellfish.
April 4, 2005	COOL labeling for fish and shellfish takes effect.
November 10, 2005	Implementation of COOL for all other covered commodities is delayed until September 30, 2008, per enactment of the FY2006 agriculture appropriations act (P.L. 109-97, §792).
May 22, 2008	Amendments to the 2002-enacted COOL provisions become law in the 2008 farm bill (P.L. 110-246, §11002), to take effect on September 30, 2008.
August 1, 2008	AMS publishes in the *Federal Register* the interim final rule to implement COOL for all covered commodities except fish and shellfish, to take effect on September 30, 2008.
December 16, 2008	Canada, joined by Mexico, holds consultations on COOL with the United States.
January 15, 2009	AMS publishes the final rule to implement COOL for all covered commodities, to take effect on March 16, 2009.
February 20, 2009	Secretary of Agriculture sends letter to meat and food industry representatives urging the voluntary adoption of three labeling changes.
March 16, 2009	COOL's final rule for all covered commodities takes effect.
June 5, 2009	Canada holds consultations with the United States to resolve differences on COOL.
October 7, 2009	Canada requests the establishment of a World Trade Organization (WTO) dispute settlement (DS) panel to consider its complaint on the U.S. COOL program. Mexico follows with a comparable request on October 9.
November 19, 2009	WTO establishes a DS panel to consider complaints made by Canada and Mexico on the U.S. COOL program.
November 18, 2011	WTO DS panel releases final report that concludes that some features of U.S. COOL discriminate against foreign livestock and are not consistent with U.S. WTO trade obligations.
March 23, 2012	The United States appeals the WTO DS panel's conclusions.
March 28, 2012	Canada and Mexico also appeal some of the DS panel's conclusions.
June 29, 2012	The WTO's Appellate Body (AB) issues its report, upholding the DS panel finding that U.S. COOL does not favorably treat imported livestock but reversing the other finding that COOL does not provide sufficient information to consumers on the origin of meat products.
July 10, 2012	The WTO's Dispute Settlement Body meets to consider approving the AB's report.

Appendix C. North American Livestock Trade

Overview

After COOL took full effect in March 2009, Canada and Mexico continued to question the trade legality of mandatory COOL, and claimed that COOL disrupted normal live cattle and hog trade patterns and caused large financial losses to their livestock industries. Canada and Mexico were concerned that labeling requirements and the need to segregate imported and domestic animals to assure proper labeling would raise the cost of handling and processing imported animals. The increased cost would ultimately lead U.S. livestock buyers to reduce live animal imports or to offer lower prices for imported animals.

The cattle and hog industries of Canada, Mexico, and the United States have become increasingly integrated over the last two decades, particularly after NAFTA took effect in 1994 and, before that, the Canada-U.S. Free Trade Agreement in 1988. These agreements, along with the global Uruguay Round Agreements under the WTO that reduced tariff and non-tariff barriers to trade, have enabled animals and animal products to move across borders more freely, based on market demand.

A number of animal health incidents have disrupted this market integration from time to time. The most significant event was the discovery of *bovine spongiform encephalopathy* (BSE or mad cow disease) in 2003, first in Canada and later in the United States, which halted most cross-border movement of cattle from Canada to the United States from mid-2003 through mid-2005. The predominance of BSE cases in Canada rather than in the United States may have contributed to wider support for the mandatory COOL law, some analysts believe, although government officials assert that both countries now have strong, scientifically defensible safeguards in place to ensure that BSE is controlled and that its infectious agent does not enter the human food supply.

Proximity, abundant feed supplies, and established feeding operations in the United States have resulted in an increase in live cattle and hog imports from Canada and Mexico. Imports may fluctuate year to year as factors such as relative animal and feed prices, inventory levels, currency exchange rates, and weather conditions influence the movement of cattle and hogs into the United States.

Canada and Mexico are important U.S. trading partners for live animals. The value of U.S. cattle and hog exports to Canada and Mexico was about $65 million in 2011 (**Table C-1**). The United States primarily exports breeding animals. In recent years, U.S. cattle and hogs have been shipped to more than 70 foreign markets, but Canada and Mexico have accounted for most of the exports.

On the import side, the value of trade with Canada and Mexico is much greater. In 2011, the United States imported more than $1.8 billion worth of cattle and hogs from Canada and Mexico (**Table C-1**). Almost all U.S. live cattle imports come from Canada and Mexico and almost all live hog imports come from Canada.

In volume terms, on average, cattle imports have accounted for about 6% of total U.S. commercial cattle slaughter since 2000. Over the same period, hog imports have accounted for nearly 7% of total hog commercial slaughter, but the hog share has dropped to 5% since 2009 as hog imports have declined from recent highs.

Table C-1. Value of U.S. Cattle and Hog Trade

($ million)

	EXPORTS				
	2007	**2008**	**2009**	**2010**	**2011**
Canada					
Cattle	15.2	9.7	13.5	19.7	39.3
Hogs	0.6	1.0	1.4	1.6	2.1
Mexico					
Cattle	15.3	51.5	25.8	30.8	20.8
Hogs	12.8	9.0	1.0	2.0	2.9
Canada & Mexico Total	44.0	71.2	41.6	54.1	65.1
World					
Cattle	48.0	108.1	58.8	132.7	375.9
Hogs	19.4	27.9	9.6	8.6	24.1

	IMPORTS				
	2007	**2008**	**2009**	**2010**	**2011**
Canada					
Cattle	1,402.8	1,462.6	917.7	1,051.9	832.3
Hogs	653.2	482.3	295.2	363.3	362.9
Mexico					
Cattle	475.5	298.3	381.0	522.8	616.9
Hogs	0.0	0.0	0.0	0.0	0.0
Canada & Mexico Total	2,531.5	2,243.1	1,593.9	1,938.0	1,812.1
World					
Cattle	1,878.3	1,760.8	1,298.7	1,574.6	1,449.2
Hogs	653.2	482.3	295.2	363.5	362.9

Source: USDA, Foreign Agricultural Service, *Global Agricultural Trade System Online.*

U.S. Cattle Imports

A majority of the cattle that Canada ships to the United States are for immediate slaughter, 84% in 2011. Most of the remaining imports are feeder cattle that are usually destined for U.S. feedlots to be fed out to slaughter-ready weights. The 15% feeder share of cattle imports in 2011 was the smallest feeder share since 2000. Declining cattle inventories combined with the availability of relatively inexpensive barley supplies in Canada during 2011 slowed shipments to the United States. A small share of Canadian imports are dairy cows and breeding stock (**Figure C-1**).

Figure C-1. U.S. Cattle Imports from Canada

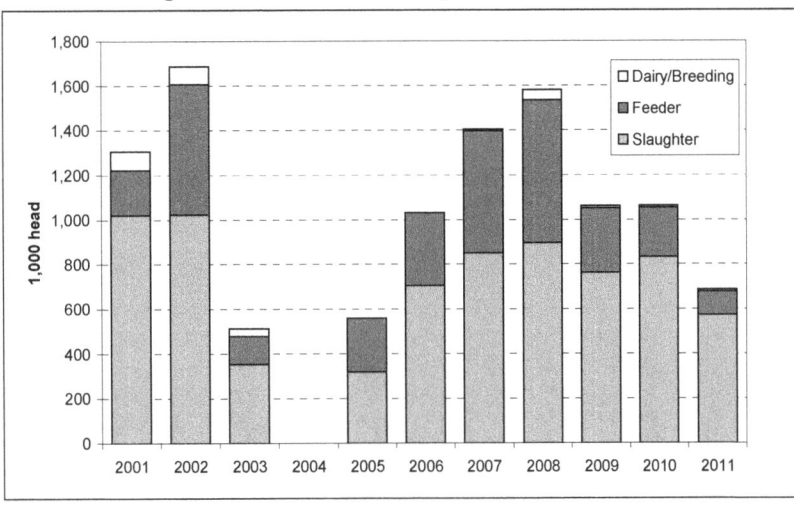

Source: USDA, Economic Research Service, "Livestock and Meat Trade Data-Cattle."

Almost 100% of Mexican cattle shipped to the United States are stocker or feeder cattle[55] that are usually raised in the northern states of Mexico, then shipped to the United States and placed on pasture or into feedlots[56] (**Figure C-2**). Cattle imports from Mexico are often influenced by prevailing precipitation conditions in northern Mexico. Persistent dryness since 2009 has led to an increasing number of cattle imports from Mexico.

Figure C-2. U.S. Cattle Imports from Mexico

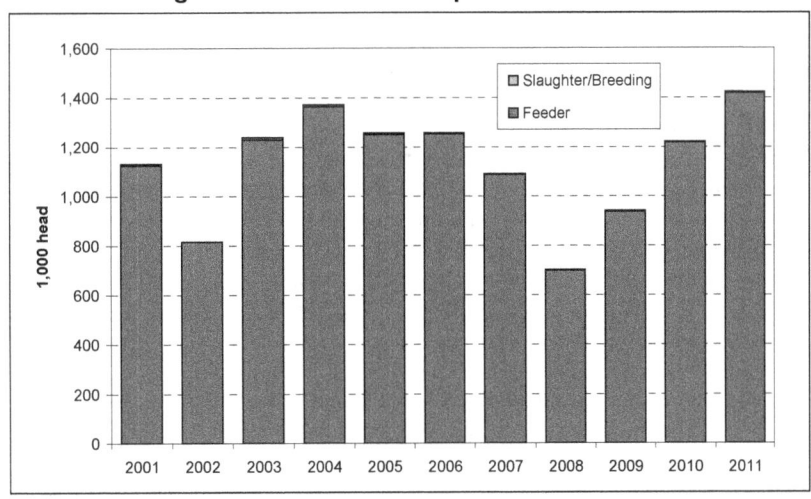

Source: USDA, Economic Research Service, "Livestock and Meat Trade Data-Cattle."

---

[55] Stocker cattle are lightweight, usually 200 to 400 pounds, and are placed in grazing programs to grow the animals. Feeder cattle are heavier, mostly 400 to 700 pounds, and may be placed on grass or placed directly in feedlots.

[56] USDA, Economic Research Service, *Trade, the Expanding Mexican Beef Industry, and Feedlot and Stocker Cattle Production in Mexico*, by Darrell S. Peel, Kenneth H. Mathews, Jr., and Rachel J. Johnson, August 2011.

U.S. cattle imports plunged in 2004 after the discovery of BSE in Canada in May 2003 and the subsequent ban on Canadian cattle imports. But once the border was reopened to Canadian cattle in 2005, imports steadily increased and reached pre-BSE levels by 2007 on a strong rebound in imports from Canada. In 2008, cattle imports dropped 8% to 2.3 million head, and fell 12% to 2 million head in 2009 (**Figure C-3**).

Figure C-3. U.S. Cattle Imports from Canada and Mexico

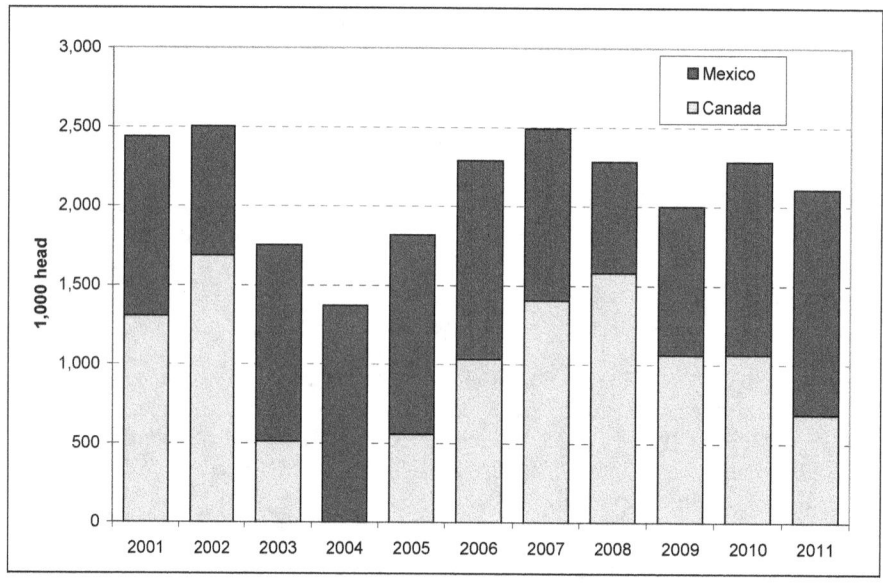

Source: USDA, Economic Research Service, "Livestock and Meat Trade Data-Cattle."

U.S. cattle imports during the first half of 2008 were almost 9% higher than the previous year, but import growth slowed during the last part of 2008, and by December cattle imports had fallen to 8% below 2007. Imports from Canada continued to grow during 2008 and imports of Canadian feeder cattle were particularly strong in the first half of the year. Under COOL regulations, cattle that were in the United States before July 15, 2008 were considered U.S. origin cattle, which likely encouraged feeder imports from Canada during the first part of the year. Canadian feeder imports through June 2008 were 72% higher than the previous year, but ended the year only 16% higher. However, during 2008 cattle imports from Mexico were 35% lower than 2007, and the lowest imports since 1998. Good range and forage conditions in Mexico allowed producers to keep cattle on grass and resulted in slower imports.

U.S. cattle imports continued to decline in 2009, but contrary to 2008, imports from Canada declined. USDA's Economic Research Service indicated that weaker cattle prices and weaker demand for beef in the United States, combined with a stronger Canadian dollar reduced Canadian returns and incentives to send cattle to the United States.[57] On the other hand, imports from Mexico started rising due to worsening drought conditions in the latter part of 2009 that encouraged Mexican producers to ship cattle to the United States.

---

[57] USDA, Economic Research Service, *Livestock, Dairy, and Poultry Outlook*, December 17, 2009. p. 5.

Some analyses attribute the import decline during the last part of 2008 and all of 2009 to COOL but differ on the extent that currency exchange rates may have contributed to this development. CattleFax, an industry-funded data and analysis service based in Colorado, observed that the 2008 decline in cattle imports was due to mandatory COOL regulations, and that imports would "face a big wild card in 2009" for the same reason.[58] Livestock sector analysts with the Chicago Mercantile Exchange (CME), examining cattle import trends through year-end 2008, commented that the COOL law "has been quite effective, if you measure effectiveness by the degree to which it has been able to stifle cattle trade in North America." They wrote that reductions in imports from both Mexico and Canada "came at a time when a significant devaluation in the value of the Peso and Canadian dollar normally would have been conducive of increased imports from these two countries. Under normal circumstances, one would expect cattle imports to actually increase rather than be cut by almost 40%."[59] However, USDA's Economic Research Service (ERS) suggested that the currency exchange factor may be somewhat more involved and that Canada's available supplies of slaughter cattle were reduced by earlier strong shipments of feeder cattle.[60]

In 2010, U.S. cattle imports increased 14% from 2009 to 2.3 million head as shipments of feeder cattle from Mexico continued to expand, due to continued drought conditions and strong U.S. feeder cattle prices that further encouraged Mexican producers to send cattle north (**Figure C-3**). Canadian cattle imports in 2010 remained flat. In 2011, total cattle imports turned down again, dropping 8% as increased imports from Mexico (+16%) were more than offset by a sharp drop in imports from Canada (-35%). Ample feed supplies last year caused more cattle to be fed in Canadian feedlots and, in addition, the relatively strong Canadian dollar dampened shipments to the United States. USDA has forecast lower cattle imports in 2012 as both Canada and Mexico ship fewer cattle.[61]

U.S. Hog Imports

U.S. hog imports from Canada have grown sharply since the mid-1990s. U.S. hog imports were a record 10 million head in 2007, growing more than 13% per year on average during the previous 10 years. Furthermore, the composition of U.S. hog imports significantly shifted from hogs for immediate slaughter to feeder pigs.[62] At one time the U.S. hog industry was comprised of many small operations that raised hogs from birth to slaughter-ready weight (farrow-to-finish operations), but from the mid-1980's the hog industry moved toward vertical integration. With vertical integration there came increased demand for feeder pigs to meet the needs of finishing operations. Some Canadian producers focused their production on providing feeder pigs for shipment to the United States where access to abundant and cheaper supplies of grain made it more economical to feed pigs to slaughter weight.[63] The feeder pig share of hog imports increased steadily from the mid-1990s, peaking at 82% in 2009, and remained stable in 2010 and 2011.

---

[58] CattleFax, "CattleFax Long Term Outlook Special Edition," December 12, 2008, p. 3.

[59] *CME Daily Livestock Report*, January 7, 2009.

[60] USDA, Economic Research Service, *Livestock, Dairy, and Poultry Outlook*, December 18, 2008, p. 8. ERS analysts point out that prior to 2008, the United States was easing the BSE-related restrictions on Canadian cattle imports; in November 2007, cattle over 30 months of age were again permitted to enter from Canada.

[61] USDA, Foreign Agricultural Service, *Livestock and Poultry World Markets and Trade*, October 2011.

[62] Feeder pigs are light-weight pigs—the majority weighing less than 15 pounds, others weighing between 15 and 100 pounds—that are shipped to the United States for feeding to slaughter-ready weight.

[63] USDA, Economic Research Service, *Market Integration of the North American Hog Industries*, November 2004, pp. (continued...)

U.S. imports of Canadian hogs have steadily declined since 2007. U.S. hog imports fell 7% in 2008 on a 30% drop in hogs for immediate slaughter. In 2009, hog imports dropped another 32% as both feeder pigs and hogs for immediate slaughter declined (**Figure C-4**).

Figure C-4. U.S. Hog Imports from Canada

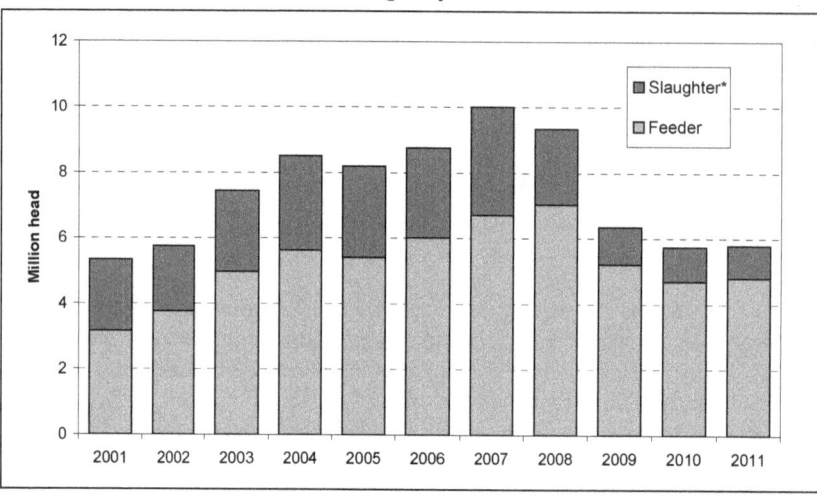

Source: USDA, Economic Research Service, "Livestock and Meat Trade Data—Hogs."

An early 2009 USDA analysis suggested that COOL's implementation likely "made U.S. swine finishers reluctant to import Canadian finishing animals, in light of some major U.S. packers' stated unwillingness to process Canadian-origin animals."[64] Another report suggested that COOL was affecting the U.S. hog sector, particularly in Iowa, as packers moved to process only U.S.-born hogs. With many Iowa producers operating finishing operations that source feeder pigs from Canada, a USDA document on COOL implementation cited that some producers' barns are "empty because of a lack of an assured outlet for slaughter hogs of mixed country of origin" (i.e., Product of Canada and United States). USDA also reported that some lenders were not extending credit to operations that finish mixed-origin pigs, and that lower prices at times were "being paid for mixed origin slaughter hogs compared to hogs of exclusively U.S. origin."[65]

In 2010, hog imports continued to decline but at a slower pace than in 2009. U.S. hog imports steadied during 2011, and totaled 5.8 million head, about 1% above 2010. USDA projects that the U.S. will import about the same number of hogs in 2012.[66]

(...continued)

9-12.

[64] USDA, Economic Research Service, *Livestock, Dairy, and Poultry Outlook*, April 16, 2009, p. 4.

[65] CattleBuyers Weekly, "MCOOL Hurts Iowa Hog Finishers," April 27, 2009.

[66] USDA, Economic Research Service, *Livestock, Dairy, and Poultry Outlook*, February 15, 2012, p. 24.

Author Contact Information

Remy Jurenas
Specialist in Agricultural Policy
rjurenas@crs.loc.gov, 7-7281

Joel L. Greene
Analyst in Agricultural Policy
jgreene@crs.loc.gov, 7-9877

Acknowledgments

This is an update of a report written by Geoffrey S. Becker, Specialist in Agricultural Policy.

www.ingramcontent.com/pod-product-compliance
Lightning Source LLC
Chambersburg PA
CBHW082201290526
45794CB00008B/3385